BUSINESS/SCIENCE/TECHNOLOGY DIVISION
CHICAGO PUBLIC LIBRARY
400 SOUTH STATE STREET
CHICAGO, IL 60605

D1088740

LOCOMOTIVES

in detail

| GRESLEY 4-6-2 | 3 | A4 CLASS |

LOCOMOTIVES

in detail

3

GRESLEY 4-6-2 A4 CLASS

DAVID CLARKE

Ian Allan
PUBLISHING

For those who know me through my association with Brassmasters, the Wild Swan series on the Class 5 and *Locomotives in Detail No 2 Stanier 4-6-0 Class 5* (with my good friend John Jennison) the fact of me producing a book on the LNER 'A4' may come as a surprise but I have always been an admirer of LNER Pacifics (of all types).

The 'A4' has one of the most distinctive shapes of any British locomotive and was a very effective tool of the operating department, earning maximum publicity for the LNER. The mystique of the class is reinforced by the stunning world speed record set in 1938 by No 60022 *Mallard* which still stands.

Their iconic status is shown by the fact that six (17% of the class) have been preserved and that three (No 60007 *Sir Nigel Gresley*, No 60009 *Union of South Africa* and No 60019 *Bittern*) are still running (or are eligible to run) on the national network. Not only does the class look good but the chime whistle is one of the most evocative sounds to emanate from a steam locomotive and once heard never forgotten.

In planning this book I have decided that for those who can still remember the 'A4' class in steam before preservation (almost 40 years ago!) I would wherever possible use the BR number as the primary reference and the LNER data would be supplementary. This presents some difficulties as the 'A4s' were renumbered more than once, many were renamed and the final BR numbers did not bear much relation to the order in which they were built.

The 'A4' from a detail point of view is a deceptively complex class with many of the detail changes being very subtle and not always easy to spot in photographs. My challenge in producing this book was to add to the information published on the class. Certainly I have spent many happy hours looking at photographs with a magnifying glass trying to identify small details and collate the information.

The objective of this series is to show to the reader the detail variations within the class in an easily understandable form and, where possible, tables have been used to summarise the as-built configuration and allow easy reference, and the text describes subsequent changes. The photographs have been chosen to show the many possible variations through the class.

For those contemplating building a model I can recommend the 4mm and 7mm models produced by Martin Finney; both capture the complex shape extremely well (which many of the 4mm proprietary examples do not). A new 7mm kit of the 'A4' has recently been released by DJH Engineering of Consett, Durham under its Piercy label. The kit contains many parts tooled by master modelmaker Tony Reynalds and from photographs it appears to assemble into a superb and accurate model.

Much of the information analysed came from the data in the Yeadon's Register for the 'A4' - it just took some time to research - and for full details of any particular locomotive this source is very useful.

Finally my thanks to John Robinson of the Severn Valley Railway for allowing access to No 60009 *Union of South Africa*.

David Clarke
Derby
February 2005

Recommended reading:

Locomotive Profile No 19, The Gresley 'A4' - Ron Scott and Brian Reed - Profile Publications December 1971.

Yeadon's Register of LNER Locomotives. Volume II, Gresley 'A4' and W1 class - Irwell Press 1990.

Profile of the A4s - J. S. Whiteley and G. W. Morrison - Oxford Publishing Co 1985 and 1999 - ISBN 0 86093 354 7

The Gresley Pacifics - O. S. Nock - David & Charles 1973.

The Power of the A4s - Brian Morrison - Oxford Publishing Co 1978, 1984, 1987, 1988 and 2002 – ISBN 0 86093 032 7

Glory Days: Gresley A4s - Gavin Morrison – Ian Allan 2001 – ISBN 0 7110 2725 0

The A4 Pacifics – P. N. Townend – Ian Allan – ISBN 0 7110 1813 8

Series Created & Edited by Jasper Spencer-Smith.
Design & Artwork: Nigel Pell.
Produced by JSS Publishing Limited, PO Box 6031, Bournemouth, BH1 9AT, England.

Title spread: No 60008 Dwight D. Eisenhower passes through Hitchin, Hertfordshire, with a down express, July 1961. (CR/BN)

First published 2005

ISBN 0 7110 3085 5

All rights reserved. No part of this book may be reproduced or transmitted in any form or by any means, electronic or mechanical, including photocopying, recording or by any information storage and retrieval system, without permission from the Publisher in writing.

© Ian Allan Publishing Ltd 2005

Published by Ian Allan Publishing

an imprint of Ian Allan Publishing Ltd, Hersham, Surrey KT12 4RG.
Printed in England by Ian Allan Printing Ltd, Hersham, Surrey KT12 4RG.

Code: 0507/B2

Photograph Credits
Colour-Rail (CR) and their photographers
C. Banks Collection (CBC); G. Ford (GF);
E. V. Fry (EVF); P. J. Hughes (PJH); N. F. Ingrams (NFI);
H. N. James (HNJ); J. M. Jarvis (JJ); H. M. Lane (HML);
National Railway Museum (NRM); Bruce Nathan (BN);
T. B. Owen (TO); K. R. Pirt (KRP); Friends of the NRM (FNR); A. C. Sterndale (ACS); D. B. Swale (DBS); George M. Staddon (GMS); J. B. Snell (JBS); R. Shenton (RSh); D. W. Webb (DWW); J. A. Whaley (JAW).
Also Gavin Morrison (GM), Rail Archive Stephenson (RAS), Ian Allan Library (IA), Author's Collection (AC).

CHICAGO PUBLIC LIBRARY   R0413298080

CONTENTS

INTRODUCTION

The streamlined shape of the locomotive
was primarily designed to improve the lifting
of exhaust steam and smoke over the casing
to ensure the driver a clear view of signals.

The genesis for the introduction of the 'A4' class came when Sir Nigel Gresley reported to the LNER Board in the spring of 1934 on the new high speed 'Flying Hamburger' service between Berlin and Hamburg, Germany which used a two-car diesel unit. Following investigations into the service and consulting the manufacturer of the railcar units, a proposal to use a turbo-charged diesel engine was made, but Gresley was reluctant to use a unit with no proven record, as the diesel engine he had seen was normally aspirated.

In parallel with the German railcar experience, the French were using the Bugatti designed two-car unit on express services and Gresley took the opportunity to travel on this a number of times and he was impressed with the way that the railcar's wedge-shaped front cut through the air.

Having seen the timings for the two continental services Gresley, in late 1934, conducted some trials with a standard 180psi boilered 'A1' Pacific to see if faster service was possible and these initial runs looked promising. Following further discussions with the London North Eastern Railway (LNER) board a second high-speed trial was run on 5 March 1935 and authority to proceed with the design of the new 'Silver Jubilee' service was given on 28 March 1935. The first 'A4' was completed on 7 September 1935 which is an incredibly short

time span for a new class of locomotive. The rapid delivery was undoubtedly assisted by Gresley and his team taking as the start point the existing 'A1' and 'A3' Pacific designs but incorporating detailed improvements. In fact most of the locomotive was similar to the 'A3' with wheels, wheelbase, motion, tender and the use of conjugated valve gear being carried forward to the new 'A4' design.

Before discussing the external shape, much of the improvements over the 'A3' class were in the refinements in the steam circuit with attention being given to the shaping and smoothing of the steam and exhaust passages. Much of this was due to Gresley's appreciation of the work of French locomotive engineer Chapelon and the result was only a 2 or 3psi drop in pressure between the boiler and the steam chest when running. This compared to the 10psi difference seen on the 'A3' thus demonstrated the efficiency of the refined steam circuit.

The streamlined shape of the locomotive was primarily designed to improve the lifting of exhaust steam and smoke over the casing to ensure the driver had a clear view of the signals. Gresley was already experimenting with various devices on the 'A3' (stack-side wing and cut-away smokebox top) to try to cure the problem of exhaust, but without much success.

No 2509 Silver Link as originally built, with inset coupling hook and shorter buffers. Also note the dust shields over each axlebox on the front axle, and the cylinder drain pipes clipped to the guard irons. (IA)

Gresley had already had to modify the shape of the 2-8-2 'P2' Mikado class with the addition of quite ugly additional deflectors and given that Gresley had a real regard for the appearance of his locomotives the streamlined casing would solve a number of problems. Streamlining should also lead to a reduction on the horsepower required to run the trains on accelerated timings, the initial estimate was that the saving would be in the region of 100 horsepower (hp) although in reality it was not quite this good.

It is likely that given the short timescales between approval and completion some work on the streamlining had been agreed before approval was given. The general shape was influenced by the Bugatti railcar but the shape was refined by work in a wind tunnel at the City & Guilds College, South Kensington, London. Tests on a wooden model were also carried out at the National Physical Laboratory. Photographs exist of another wooden mock up of the

front portion of the casing which details some features not carried through to the first locomotive. These included the fitting of streamlined front lamps.

The streamlined shape also presented a problem in how to engineer a working arrangement to open the front of the casing to allow access to the smokebox door. This was eventually resolved by the use of two flat doors in the casing (known as the 'cods mouth'). The design was allegedly inspired by the draughtsman responsible for this part after he observed a waste disposal vehicle at work on the streets of Doncaster whilst on his way to the office.

The design of the chimney also underwent some changes from that originally envisaged as the top of the chimney was originally intended to carry the casing back to the level of the boiler to make a straight line from the top to the cab roof. However wind tunnel work proved this to be unsatisfactory.

Left:
No 2509 Silver Link as originally built with short buffers and recessed front coupling. It is painted in the striking grey and silver livery. Note the painted name. Only one central cab ventilator is fitted. The two additional vents were added circa 1937. (IA)

Left:
No 60027 Merlin at Perth in August 1963 showing the plaque HMS Merlin on the side of the boiler casing. Note the three open vents on the cab roof.
(G. W. Sharpe / AC)

CHAPTER ONE

DESIGN

The staff at LNER's Doncaster works took what they knew worked and made detailed changes, so to many of the draughtsmen the 'A4' was really a 'super A3' but with streamlining.

The start point for the design team at Doncaster was the 'A3' Pacific which was a development of the 'A1' class. The lesson learnt from the exchange trial with the Great Western Railway (GWR) a few years earlier was that small details (such as valve travel, also lap and lead settings) could make a significant improvement to the performance of a locomotive. The staff at Doncaster drawing office took what they knew worked and made detailed changes, so to many the 'A4' was really a 'super A3' but with streamlining.

The items that the 'A4' shared with the 'A3' were as follows:

- Three cylinders with two sets of outside Walschaerts valve gear with the inside cylinder linked by conjugated valve gear
- Wheels and wheelbase
- Boiler
- Tender

Commencing with the boiler, the base component was that of the 'A3', but with the addition of a combustion chamber which reduced the length of the boiler tubes but increased the firebox heating area. The superheater area was also increased and the boiler pressure was raised from 220 to 250psi. The result was a very free steaming boiler, helped by revisions made to the firebars and ashpan which ensured a good flow of air through the grate and firebox. The boiler diameter of the 'A3' was retained and the external dimensions of the two boilers were the same, so that when additional spare 'A4' boilers were made in the 1950s (and up to 1960) some were also fitted to 'A3s' at times (boiler pressure was reduced to 220psi when fitted to an 'A3'). The preserved 'A3', No 4472 *Flying Scotsman* is currently running with an 'ex-A4' reduced pressure boiler.

The design of the cylinders and valve gear closely followed that of the 'A3', three cylinders with conjugated valve gear with cross levers from the two outside motions providing the drive to the inside piston valve. The cylinders were also modified from that of the 'A3' with a small reduction in cylinder diameter (down from 19in [48.26cm] to 18.5in [46.99cm]) but with the piston valve size increasing from 8in (20.32cm) to 9in (22.86cm). By careful shaping and refining of the steam passages, ports and exhaust passages the locomotives were very strong and free running.

The frames and running gear also closely followed the 'A3' design but with revisions to the axlebox spring length and to the deflection rates. Also the wheels were checked on a machine at Doncaster for centrifugal balance at a speed of 80mph (128.7km/h). The result was a locomotive with excellent riding characteristics at speed.

Above:
No 60033 Seagull in ex-works condition at Doncaster, August 1959. It is painted in the final BR Brunswick Green and with the later totem. Interestingly there are no overhead power warning flashes; these were fitted in 1961. (CR/PH)

Left:
The double chimney. The ring holes behind the two exhausts are for the snifting valve that is fitted underneath. This valve allowed air to enter the super-heater elements when the regulator was closed. (GM)

Above:
The 2-8-2 Class 'P2' No 2001 Cock O' The North as originally built in 1934 with large deflectors in an attempt to keep the exhaust clear of the cab. (IA)

Right:
'P2' class No 2003 Lord President as built in June 1936 with a streamlined front similar to the 'A4's' which was far superior for lifting the exhaust. (IA)

British Railways Number	Final Name	Date Built	Original Number	1946 LNER Number	Works Number	Double Chimney Fitted	Advance Warning System	Speed Recorder (Smith-Stone type)	With-drawn
60001	Sir Ronald Matthews	26/04/38	4500	1	1873	11/04/58	09/01/59	05/10/61	10/64
60002	Sir Murrough Wilson	12/04/38	4499	2	1872	18/07/57	26/03/59	26/01/61	05/64
60003	Andrew K. McCosh	12/08/37	4494	3	1859	05/07/57	19/04/50	02/02/61	12/62
60004	William Whitelaw	10/12/37	4462	4	1864	05/12/57	13/11/58	25/01/61	07/66
60005	Sir Charles Newton	08/06/38	4901	5	1875	From new	10/12/58	14/07/60	03/64
60006	Sir Ralph Wedgwood	26/01/38	4466	6	1868	25/09/57	01/11/50	29/12/60	09/65
60007	Sir Nigel Gresley	30/10/37	4498	7	1863	13/12/57	27/09/50	16/04/59	02/66
60008	Dwight D. Eisenhower	04/09/37	4496	8	1861	20/08/58	23/06/50	30/06/60	07/63
60009	Union of South Africa	17/04/37	4488	9	1853	18/11/58	17/02/60	17/02/60	06/66
60010	Dominion of Canada	04/05/37	4489	10	1854	27/12/57	29/09/50	15/10/60	05/65
60011	Empire of India	25/06/37	4490	11	1855	11/01/58	22/10/58	28/06/60	05/64
60012	Commonwealth of Australia	22/06/37	4491	12	1856	28/07/58	19/03/59	27/10/61	08/64
60013	Dominion of New Zealand	27/06/37	4492	13	1857	04/07/58	06/11/52	29/06/61	04/63
60014	Silver Link	07/09/35	2509	14	1818	30/10/57	28/09/50	12/04/61	12/62
60015	Quicksilver	21/09/35	2510	15	1819	19/08/57	11/02/53	13/01/61	04/63
60016	Silver King	05/11/35	2511	16	1821	13/06/57	19/08/59	08/07/60	03/65
60017	Silver Fox	18/02/35	2512	17	1823	18/05/57	21/09/50	26/10/60	10/63
60018	Sparrow Hawk	27/11/37	4463	18	1864	05/10/57	19/11/58	17/02/61	06/63
60019	Bittern	18/12/37	4464	19	1866	06/09/57	13/12/58	16/03/60	09/66
60020	Guillemot	08/01/38	4465	20	1867	07/11/57	06/11/58	19/05/61	03/64
60021	Wild Swan	19/02/38	4467	21	1869	30/04/58	31/03/50	17/11/61	10/63
60022	Mallard	03/03/38	4468	22	1870	From new	10/02/53	09/03/60	04/63
60023	Golden Eagle	22/12/35	4482	23	1847	18/09/58	23/03/59	10/06/60	10/64
60024	Kingfisher	26/12/38	4483	24	1848	20/08/58	15/06/61	10/06/60	09/66
60025	Falcon	23/01/37	4484	25	1849	04/09/58	27/01/50	16/06/60	10/63
60026	Miles Beevor	20/02/37	4485	26	1850	15/08/57	30/10/50	21/10/60	12/65
60027	Merlin	13/03/37	4486	27	1851	02/02/58	19/05/60	19/05/60	09/65
60028	Walter K. Whigham	20/03/37	4487	28	1852	02/11/57	13/10/50	18/04/61	12/62
60029	Woodcock	26/07/37	4493	29	1858	03/10/58	17/10/50	08/04/60	10/63
60030	Golden Fleece	30/08/37	4495	30	1860	15/05/58	15/01/53	28/07/61	12/62
60031	Golden Plover	02/10/37	4497	31	1862	11/03/58	13/05/60	15/03/61	10/65
60032	Gannet	17/05/38	4900	32	1874	27/11/58	20/02/53	29/04/60	10/63
60033	Seagull	28/06/38	4902	33	1876	From new	25/02/53	08/06/61	12/62
60034	Lord Faringdon	01/07/38	4903	34	1877	From new	11/11/52	02/11/60	08/66
	Gadwall	30/03/38	4469		1871	Never Fitted	Never Fitted	Never fitted	06/42

Left:
No 2001 Cock O' The North after the original smoke deflectors were replaced with an 'A4' style front in April 1938. The valve gear has also been changed from poppet valves to standard piston valve gear. (NRM)

CHAPTER TWO

CONSTRUCTION

With the exception of liveries and tenders 'A4' locomotives
were almost identical and it was only over the ensuing years
that more obvious changes took place.

The first locomotive, No 60014 *Silver Link,*
was completed in three months between
26 June and September 1935. It was
followed by three more in quick succession:
No 60015 *Quicksilver*, No 60016 *Silver King* and
No 60017 *Silver Fox* in October, November and
December 1935 respectively.

Before any further locomotives were ordered,
the performance of the first four was monitored
but Doncaster had nothing to worry about as the
'A4' class was demonstrably better than the 'A1'
and 'A3' Pacifics on the haulage of heavy trains on
scheduled services then in force. In January 1936,
approval was given for the construction of an
additional 17 locomotives and in October 1936
the order to build a further 14 was given. The first
completed locomotive following these orders was
No 60023 *Golden Eagle* (as No 4482) in December
1936 and 'A4s' were being delivered at almost
monthly intervals during 1937 and 1938 with the
last, No 60034 *Lord Faringdon* (then as No 4903
Peregrine), completed in July 1938.

With the exception of liveries and tenders
the 'A4s' were almost identical.

FRONT BUFFERS & COUPLINGS

The first four built – *Silver Link, Quicksilver, Silver
King* and *Silver Fox* – were fitted with short
buffer stocks and a recessed pocket for the

coupling hook. All had a different radius to the
bottom of the streamlined casing (allegedly the
result of misreading of the correct dimensions
for the radius on work's drawings). The short-
stock buffers made coupling hazardous work for
yard staff and following a fatality the buffer
stocks were lengthened. The casing around the
coupling was modified in 1936. All locomotives
subsequently built carried these modifications.

CHIMNEYS

The locomotives were originally fitted with
single chimney but in 1938 No 60022 (as
No 4468) *Mallard* was fitted with a double
chimney and subsequently the last were built
new with the double chimney (No 60005
Sir Charles Newton, No 60033 *Seagull* and
No 60034 *Lord Faringdon*). Despite the benefits
to steaming it is surprising that it was only
from 1957 that the remainder of the class were
converted to double chimney. Gresley had
plans in 1939 to fit the rest of the class but this
was overtaken by the outbreak of World War
Two in 1939. The last conversion to No 60009
Union of South Africa was completed in
November 1958. The chimney was of the
Kylchap type which gave a very distinctive soft
exhaust but was highly effective in reducing
back pressure. p.18 ▶

No 60034 Lord Faringdon in its final condition, showing the Advanced Warning System (AWS) 'bang' plate which protects the contact shoe from the front coupling. Note also the polished buffer heads and the 'curly' numeral six on the smokebox numberplate. (GM)

Right:
No 4462 William Whitelaw showing the front casing still in place whilst the skirting panel over the driving wheels had been removed, June 1941. (IA)

Right:
The 'cods-mouth' door has been removed (along with the outer chimney casing.
(Malcolm Slater / AC)

Left:
No 4487 Sea Eagle
with the original
valancing removed
during World War
Two. (IA)

Left:
The half dust shields
as originally fitted
to No 2509
Silver Jubilee. (RAS)

Left:
Full-width shields,
also the cylinder
drain pipes in the
original position
clipped to the
front guard irons
(No 60007 Sir Nigel
Gresley, 1947). (RAS)

Left:
Here the dust shield
has been cut to allow
the AWS contact
shoe to be fitted.
The front guard irons
are removed and the
drain pipes shortened
(No 60022 Mallard,
1954) (AC)

Front Guard Irons & Cylinder Drain Cocks

The 'A4' as built had double pairs of guard irons, a long pair attached to the mainframes and a shorter pair on the bogie. The cylinder drainpipes extended forward and were clipped to the longer guard irons.

The removal of the long guard irons attached to the mainframes began in December 1952 (No 60025 *Falcon*) and continued when locomotives went for heavy repair, with the last irons being removed in June 1954 (No 60013 *Dominion of New Zealand*). This coincided with the fitment of the Advance Warning System (AWS) and it can be assumed that the long guard irons made the fitment of this equipment more difficult.

The removal of the long guard irons necessitated the shortening of the cylinder drain pipes and this was carried out when the guard irons were modified.

Valve Gear

The Walschaerts valve gear broadly followed existing LNER practice, and had a two-piece expansion link bolted together with two bronze die blocks and four-stud fixing for the return crank.

In the British Railways (BR) period the coupling and connecting rods were changed from the elegant '**I**' section (in nickel-chrome steel) to a sturdier '**I**' section in carbon steel. This was the result of a number of failures of coupling rods on a number of ex-LNER classes.

Bogie Dust Shields

At various times the 'A4' (along with the 'A3') had dust shields fitted at the front of the bogie. The style varied, sometimes full width and sometimes only just inside the wheels. Many locomotives were fitted with each type at various times whilst in service. The full-width dust shields were finally removed when the locomotives were fitted with AWS, although during some of the early installations of this equipment, in the 1950s, dust shields were still fitted but with a cut out slot in the middle of the shield to accommodate the AWS contact shoe. p.24 ▶

Left:
No 60010 Dominion
of Canada in final
condition complete
with overhead power
warning flashes.
Note the absence
of a works plate on
the cab side; this
was fitted on the
inside. (GM)

Below:
No 60014 Silver Link
at Grantham with an
up express. (CR/KRP)

Right:
No 4459 Golden
Shuttle in blue livery
with the stainless-
steel trim strip along
the bottom of the
valance and lower
edge of the tender.
It is also fitted with
stainless-steel
numbers and
letters. (IA)

Left:
No 4496 Golden Shuttle, now re-named Dwight D. Eisenhower, still in blue livery but now with the valance panels removed. The tender retains the backing strip for the stainless-steel strip which has now been removed. The locomotive is fitted with stainless-steel numbers and letters. Note the shed name (Grantham) painted on the buffer beam. (IA)

Above:
The cylinder drain pipes were cut back when the guard irons were modified. (AC)

Right:
No 4498 Sir Nigel Gresley in 1993. The two mechanical lubricators are driven from the rear driving wheels. (AC)

Above:
The valve gear and motion which appears almost too delicate to operate such a powerful locomotive. (AC)

Left:
The Cartazi-type trailing truck. Note the rods for operating the dampers under the firebox. (AC)

Examples of locomotives fitted with shields are as follows:

Number	Type	Date
60003	two small	1938 and 1950
60004	full width	1952
60005	two small	1939
60008	two small	1939
60009	full width	1954
60010	full width	1949
60011	two small	1939
60012	full width	1956
60013	two small	
60014	two small	1936 and 1953
60016	full width	1939 and 1958
60017	two small	1937 and 1951
60019	full width	1950
60021	full width	1949
60022	full width	1954
60024	full width	1957
60026	full width	1950
60027	full width	1949
60028	two small	1953
60030	full width	1953
60031	full width	1950
60032	two small	1954
60033	two small	1952
60034	two small	1950s

SPEED INDICATORS

LNER experimented with speedometers on a number of classes from the late 1930s. All the 'A4s' were fitted with Flamon (of French origin) speed recorders, mounted on an inverted 'A' frame above the right-hand side trailing wheel. At the point of the 'A' frame a small gearbox was fitted and was driven from the coupling rod via a crankpin. A horizontal rod transmitted the drive to the recorder located under the driver's seat where the speed was registered on a paper sheet.

During the war problems with the supply of paper rolls meant that all the recorders were removed. After the end of the war in 1945 the locomotives used in the Exchange trials (No 60022 *Mallard*, No 60033 *Seagull* and No 60034 *Lord Faringdon*) had the equipment re-fitted in 1948. By 1951 others had been re-fitted including No 60003 *Andrew K. McCosh*, No 60006 *Sir Ralph Wedgwood*, No 60009 *Union of South Africa*, No 60011 *Empire of India*, No 60012 *Commonwealth of Australia*, No 60026 *Miles Beevor*, No 60024 *Kingfisher*, No 60027

Merlin and No 60029 *Woodcock*. However the equipment was again taken off and by 1952 only No 60022 *Mallard* and No 60023 *Golden Eagle* still carried the speed recorder.

The BR standard Smith–Stone speed indicator was fitted to all 'A4s' between April 1959 (No 60007 *Sir Nigel Gresley*) and November 1961 (No 60021 *Wild Swan*). The fitment consisted of a small electric generator driven from the left-hand trailing crankpin. A curved-shape electric conduit connected the generator to a cab-mounted speedometer for the driver.

Above:
No 60019 Bittern at Darlington works in March 1965, its last visit before returning to Scotland for a further 12 months' service. Clearly seen is the bracket for the reversing handle.
(Ian G. Holt)

CHAPTER THREE

RUNNING PLATE & CAB

The layout of the 'A4' cab changed little during the service life of the class. Backhead fitments remained standard whilst ventilation was improved by fitting vents in the cab roof.

The first five locomotives (*Silver Link*, *Quicksilver*, *Silver King*, *Silver Fox* and *Golden Eagle*, and possibly *Kingfisher*, *Falcon*, *Kestrel*, *Merlin* and *Sea Eagle*) were built with a single ventilator in the centre of the cab roof. From photographic evidence it would appear that two additional ventilators on both sides of the roof were added from 1937.

AWS EQUIPMENT

With the installation of automatic train control equipment on the main line between King's Cross (King's +) shed and Grantham shed several 'A4s' were fitted with Advance Warning System (AWS) commencing with No 60025 *Falcon* in January 1950. When the system was extended further north to York all the 'A4s' were subsequently fitted although some of the Scottish-based locomotives were not fitted until 1960.

The fitment of AWS could be identified as follows:
- Contact shoe attached to the front of the bogie.
- 'Bash' plate fitted to prevent the front coupling swinging back and damaging the contact shoe.
- Pipe clipped to the left-hand valance platform and running along this and then under the cab.

SIDE SKIRTING

As originally built the side skirting covered most of the motion. However under war conditions it was deemed appropriate to remove both the skirting covering the wheels and that covering the space in front of the cylinders (allowing better access to parts of the conjugated valve gear, which required regular maintenance).

In July 1941 No 60004 (as No 4462) *William Whitelaw* had the skirting covering the driving wheels removed but the valance panel in front of the cylinders was retained. The valance was modified so that it hinged and was secured by stud fasteners. However at the same time No 60023 (as No 4482) *Golden Eagle* and No 60028 *Walter K. Whigham* (as No 4487 *Sea Eagle*) had the valance in front of the cylinders and the skirting over the driving wheels completely removed. The remaining 'A4s' were dealt with as they passed through works, the last three in September 1942. The modified No 60004 had the valence in front of the cylinders removed in October 1942 (rumoured to have been completed at Haymarket shed).

HANDRAIL

As built in 1935 on No 60014 *Silver Link* (running as No 2509) the handrail on the boiler casing

The driver's side of No 60009 Union of South Africa. The handle in front of the seat is the reverser. The seats are a distinct improvement to those fitted to many other classes of locomotive and reflected the long-distance work to be performed. (AC)

Above:
The Crosby 'Tri-Tone' whistle. (RAS)

Right:
The cab and back-head of No 2509 Silver Link as built. Subsequently two additional vents were fitted in the cab roof. A different type of seat (better upholstered) was fitted in later years. (RAS)

continued in a horizontal line to the firebox end (on all the other 'A4s' the handrail curved down). This was changed to conform with all the class when the locomotive was repainted blue in December 1937.

WHISTLES

The standard fitment on the 'A4s' was the Crosby 'Tri-Tone' (known as a chime whistle) which originated from the USA. This was 4in (10.16cm) in diameter and was easily identifiable when fitted (as in the above photograph).

During World War Two these were removed as it was thought that the sound could be confused with that of air raid sirens and were replaced by the standard single note LNER-type whistle (much smaller than the chime type). However not all were removed and the following retained the chime whistle:

No 60006 Sir Ralph Wedgwood
(running as No 4466)
No 60025 Falcon
(running as No 4484)
No 60028 Walter K. Whigham
(running as No 4487)

After the war ended the chime whistles were re-installed but this took some time with the last being fitted in 1948.

Not all locomotives retained the chime whistle and the following lists other types fitted to the 'A4s':

No 60009 Union of South Africa: fitted with a South African Railways-type whistle.

No 60010 Dominion of Canada: fitted with a Canadian Pacific Railway Company (CPR) whistle before World War Two, but this was removed in 1949. It was to form part of a whistles trial for the proposed BR Standard Class locomotives carried out at Stratford. It was replaced by a standard chime whistle and the CPR whistle was never refitted.

No 60012 Commonwealth of Australia: fitted in 1960 with a large diameter multi-tone whistle, from a Western Australian Railways locomotive, supplied by Captain Howey of the Romney, Hythe & Dymchurch Railway.

No 60013 Dominion of New Zealand: fitted with a New Zealand Government Railways-type whistle in 1939 (as No 4492). The sound of the whistle was five notes of a lower pitch than the more usual chime type.

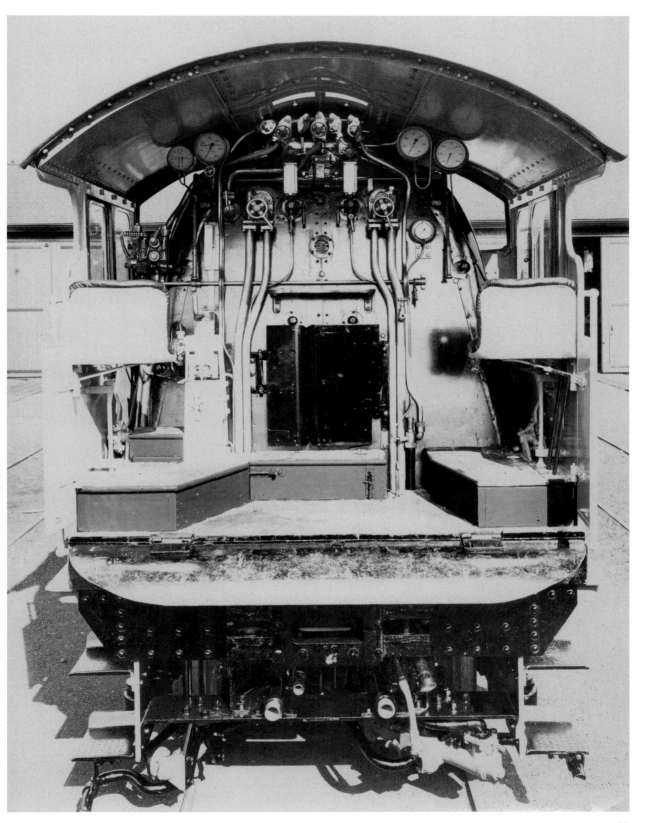

CHAPTER FOUR

TENDERS

All the tenders were of 5,000 gallons water capacity and carried 9 tons of coal. The weight of the tender varied between 60.6 tons and 65.6 tons.

Tenders for the 'A4' class can be divided into two main types but with some detail differences within each type as follows:

CORRIDOR TENDERS

Streamline corridor tender (built new)
The tenders fitted to the first four locomotives delivered in 1935 were similar to the tenders built in 1928 for the non-stop 'Flying Scotsman' service but had additional curved end and top fairings at the front and rear, also additional curving of the sides (at the top), but did not have any raised beading on the side sheets. (Tender numbers were Nos 5589 to 5592.) In 1939 one of these tenders (No 5590) was fitted with Timken roller bearings. Two further tenders were fitted with other manufacturers' roller bearings during the same period.

An additional seven tenders to the same design as Nos 5589 to 5592 were built in 1937 and numbered 5646 to 5652 and fitted to locomotives Nos 4491 to 4497. One of the tenders (No 5647) was fitted with Hoffman roller bearings in 1939. Six of these tenders also had a stainless steel strip fitted to the edge of the tender footplate to match that of the stainless strip at the edge of the side skirting on the locomotive. When this was removed the strip on the tender was painted

over. This can be noted on tenders up until withdrawal from service.

1928 Pattern corridor altered to streamline in 1937 and 1938
Chronologically the next tender type and fitted to the 'A4' were rebuilds of corridor tenders previously fitted to the 'A3'. These tenders were given 'streamlined' sides and fairings, raised front coal plates and disc wheels in place of the original spoked type. All retained the straight back plate and beading along the top of the sides and back. Eleven of these tenders were built in 1937/38.

NON CORRIDOR TENDERS

Five new non-corridor tenders were built in 1937 and an additional nine were built in 1937/38. This second batch of tenders was built without the top fairings at the back end. Earlier tenders had this fairing removed in 1938, and external appearance was similar to the streamlined corridor tenders and did not have raised beading (as per the 1928-pattern corridor tenders).

Two of the tenders used in the 1948 Locomotive Trials were modified to allow the use of alternative coalers (the modification consisted of cutting down the top fairing to

Rear of a streamline corridor tender, showing the buck-eye coupling fitted to these tenders in the 'stowed' position allowing the hook to be used with non- buck-eye equipped stock. (IA)

Number	Built With	Changed to	Changed to	Change
60001	Non Corridor			
60002	Non Corridor			
60003	Streamline Corridor	Non Corridor, 1952/4	1928 Pattern Streamline Corridor, 1954/5	Non Corridor, 1955-62
60004	Non Corridor	1928 Pattern Streamline Corridor, 1941-66		
60005	Non Corridor			
60006	Non Corridor	Streamline Corridor, 1951/53	Streamline Corridor, 1953/4	Non Corridor, 1954-65
60007	1928 Pattern Streamline Corridor, 1941-66			
60008	Streamline Corridor	Non Corridor, 1957-63		
60009	1928 Pattern Streamline Corridor	Streamline Corridor 1948-63		
60010	1928 Pattern Streamline Corridor			
60011	1928 Pattern Streamline Corridor			
60012	Streamline Corridor			
60013	Streamline Corridor	Non Corridor, 1951/55	Streamline Corridor, 1955-63	
60014	Streamline Corridor			
60015	Streamline Corridor			
60016	Streamline Corridor	Non Corridor, 1948-65		
60017	Streamline Corridor			
60018	Non Corridor			
60019	Non Corridor			
60020	Non Corridor			
60021	Non Corridor	Streamline Corridor, 1957-63		
60022	Non Corridor	1928 Pattern Streamline Corridor		
60023	1928 Pattern Streamline Corridor	Non Corridor, 1941-64		
60024	1928 Pattern Streamline Corridor	Non Corridor, 1966		
60025	1928 Pattern Streamline Corridor	Streamline Corridor, 1958-63		
60026	1928 Pattern Streamline Corridor	Non Corridor, 1952/53	1928 Pattern Streamline Corridor	Non Corridor, 1954-65
60027	1928 Pattern Streamline Corridor	Streamline Corridor, 1948-65		
60028	1928 Pattern Streamline Corridor	Non Corridor, 1951/52	Streamline Corridor, 1952-62	
60029	Streamline Corridor	1928 Pattern Streamline Corridor		
60030	Streamline Corridor	Non Corridor, 1948-51	1928 Pattern Streamline Corridor	
60031	Streamline Corridor			
60032	Non Corridor	1928 Pattern Streamline Corridor	Non Corridor, 1953/54	Streamline Corridor, 1954/55
60033	Non Corridor	1928 Pattern Streamline Corridor		
60034	Non Corridor	1928 Pattern Streamline Corridor	Non Corridor, 1963/66	
4469	Non Corridor			

allow a bucket coaler to swing over the tender for loading) on other regions and these tenders retained this modification until withdrawal, No 5323 fitted to No 60033 *Seagull* and No 5332 fitted to No 60034 *Lord Faringdon*.

All the tenders were of 5,000 gallons (22,720 litres) water capacity and carried 9 tons (9,144.4kg) of coal. The weight of the tender varied between 60.6 tons (61,572kg) and 65.6 tons (66,652.33kg).

TENDER EXCHANGES

Over the years some tenders were exchanged but many locomotives retained the original tender fitted until withdrawal from service.

The allocation of the locomotive would dictate which type of tender would be attached, for example the diagrams from Gateshead shed did not require a corridor tender so all the locomotives allocated had non-corridor tenders.

No 60024 *Kingfisher* had a very late tender change when this unit was exchanged with the then withdrawn *Lord Faringdon* (stored at Perth at that time) in August 1966 with *Kingfisher* being withdrawn in September 1966. Such tender changes were not uncommon towards the end of steam services and often allowed locomotives to remain in traffic.

Above:
Streamline corridor tender fitted to No 60009 Union of South Africa. Note the two cab ventilators visible and the sheeting between cab roof and tender. (IA)

Above:
The 1928 Pattern
corridor tender fitted
to No 60024
Kingfisher at
Haymarket shed,
Edinburgh, 1964. (AC)

Right:
Streamline corridor
tender fitted to
No 60017 Silver Fox
in the early 1960s.
(Eric Treacy)

Above:
Top of the tender on No 60009 Union of South Africa. This is a 1928 Pattern which was refurbished and streamlined in 1937/38. (AC)

Left:
One of the 1928 Pattern (11 built) corridor tenders previously fitted to the 'A1'/'A3' classes and refurbished in 1937/38 to fit to the 'A4s'. The streamlined cover around the water filler was removed in 1938. (IA)

Left:
Down 'Flying Scotsman' service leaving Newcastle hauled by No 60004 William Whitelaw. The tender is a 1928 Pattern corridor, 'streamlined' when refurbished and fitted to 'A4s' in 1937/38. Most obvious is the raised beading on this batch of tenders. Note the early version of BR totem.
(Eric Treacy)

CHAPTER FIVE

LIVERIES & NAMES

After World War Two the majority of the Class A4 locomotives
were returned to the pre-war glory of blue livery.
Over the ensuing years many colour schemes were
tried until all were painted in BR Brunswick Green.

Liveries used on the 'A4' is a complex subject and some locomotives appeared in six different liveries throughout service (as an example No 60024 *Kingfisher* appeared in LNER Green, LNER Garter Blue (twice), LNER Black, BR Purple and BR Green). The reason for many of the initial livery variations was prompted by the desire to use groups of locomotives for specific services, so the first four were painted in Dark Grey and Silver to match the coaching stock of the 'Silver Jubilee' service. Similarly those in Garter Blue were used on the 'Coronation' service.

LIVERIES

LNER Grey. The livery in fact used three shades of grey (silver, battleship and charcoal). Wheels were silver with grey tyres. Numbers and letters were silver with blue shading. Only four locomotives were painted in this livery (*Silver Link*, *Quicksilver*, *Silver King* and *Silver Fox*). Before entering traffic *Silver Link* was photographed in the yard at Doncaster works without the parabolic curve of the black smokebox and the whole of the side in grey (and with a cast nameplate). The flat front of the smokebox was painted black but the nameplate was removed and the smokebox painted in the more recognised style by the time *Silver Link* entered traffic. Allegedly one of Gresley's daughters thought that the projecting

nameplate spoiled the complete streamlined effect so it was removed and the name was painted on the casing.

LNER Green. Lined in white and black. The smokebox was painted with the parabolic curve on the leading end. Lettering was gold with red shading. The livery was intended to run with trains of teak coaches.

LNER Green. Introduced in December 1936. Similar to above but with the green paint cut back to a vertical line to the boiler strip just behind the chimney. This style was only used on *Kingfisher*, *Falcon*, *Kestrel*, *Merlin* and *Sea Eagle* it was retained until the next overhaul some 12 months later.

LNER Garter Blue. The only lining was at the front where the black of the smokebox and the Garter Blue was separated by a red and white line, again in a parabolic curve. The wheel centres were finished in dark red. The locomotive frames and tender frames were in black. There were some differences in detail when painted blue, some (Nos 2509 to 2512) had silver transfers shaded red and black. Others had stainless steel letters and numbers on the cab side and tender. Subsequently these on later locomotives when painted blue were replaced with transfers. After World War Two the majority of the 'A4s' were returned to the glory of blue livery, and after the formation of British Railways had this title

Above:
No 4489 Dominion of Canada in Garter Blue livery outside the paintshop at Doncaster, March 1938. Note the stainless steel strip at the bottom of the valance and tender. Also note the coat of arms for Canada on the cabside and the CPR-type bell in front of the chimney. (CR/FNR)

Left:
No 2511 Silver King in blue livery and fitted with red-backed nameplates. It does not have the stainless steel trim usually fitted to the lower edge of the skirting. The location is King's Cross yard, 1938. (CR/NRM)

Right:
When new No 4489 Woodcock ran for two weeks in paintshop grey with green wheels. The locomotive went back to Doncaster to be re-painted in blue and re-named Dominion of Canada. Seen here in the short-lived grey livery. (RAS)

Below:
No 2512 Silver Fox in the grey and silver livery of the first four 'A4s' but embellished with stainless steel boiler bands and a cast stainless steel fox on the centre of the boiler casing. (IA)

painted in cream in full on the tender side replacing 'LNER'.

The five locomotives built for the 'Coronation' service – No 60009 (as No 4488) *Union of South Africa*, No 60010 (as No 4489) *Woodcock*, No 60011 (as No 4490) *Empire of India*, No 60012 (as No 4491) *Commonwealth of Australia*, No 60013 (as No 4492) *Dominion of New Zealand* and No 60007 (as No 4498) *Sir Nigel Gresley* – had a polished stainless steel strip along the bottom edges of the side skirting and tender. When the locomotives were re-painted blue this strip was removed from the skirting but not from the tender.

LNER Black. Wartime conditions led to the painting of locomotives in plain black with no lining but with 'LNER' or 'NE' in gold, shaded with red on the tender.

BR Purple. Part of the experiments to determine the new-style BR liveries. In June and July 1948, four 'A4s' (*Kingfisher, Merlin. Walter K. Whigham* and *Woodcock*) were painted

in a shade of blue which had a purple hue and was finished with distinctive lining in red/cream/ grey, and 'British Railways' in cream on the tender. The lining differed from what had been used before, being painted on the valance edge and continuing round the front of the streamlining.

BR Blue. From May 1949 all 'A4s' were painted in BR blue lined out in black and white. A new-style lion and wheel (also known as the ferret and dartboard) totem was painted on the tender. The last 'A4' to receive this livery was No 60033 *Seagull* in December 1950.

BR Brunswick Green. From August 1951 the livery was changed to Brunswick Green lined out in orange and black. This became the standard livery for all express locomotives in service on all regions. Initially the early lion and wheel totem was used. From mid-1957 this was changed to the later-style totem. All the 'A4s' received this livery and one of the last changed from BR blue was No 60017 *Silver Fox* in December 1951.

Top:
No 4901 Charles Newton in wartime all-black livery, 1942. (IA)

Above:
No 4482 Golden Eagle, the first 'A4' to be painted in LNER green lined in black and white. This livery was only applied to eight 'A4s'. Note the absence of the additional cab ventilators. (IA)

No 60026 *Miles Beevor* (*Kestrel*) was the last to be repainted green in January 1953.

The Doncaster shed interpretation of the BR green livery was that all the boiler bands (with the exception of the one over the middle of the firebox) were lined. However when Darlington shed took over responsibility for overhauls after 1963, No 60019 *Bittern* was seen with this middle firebox band lined (possibly after a heavy intermediate overhaul in 1965) and ran like this until withdrawn. Similarly No 60034 *Lord Faringdon* was observed around 1965/66 with the firebox boiler band lined out. (The locomotive had also been at Darlington in 1965 for a heavy intermediate overhaul.)

From April 1960, following continental practice, BR fitted white enamel plates with the symbolic warning sign of forked lightning (in red) to strategic positions on the boiler casing to warn of the danger of contact with overhead power wires. This was a strange fitment to the 'A4s' as the class virtually never ran under these wires in normal service. The position of the plates varied from one locomotive to another.

NAMEPLATES

The first four locomotives built in 1935 (*Silver Link*, *Quicksilver*, *Silver King* and *Silver Fox*) did not have nameplates but had the name painted on the side of the boiler casing and only received cast

nameplates in 1937. Although a photograph exists showing *Silver Link* fitted with a nameplate in the more usual position, it was removed before the locomotive entered traffic. Presumably the same plate was used when the nameplate was refitted in December 1937 when *Silver Link* was repainted blue.

The nameplates were attached to the side of the smokebox, and the background colour was usually black, and were normally fitted with the front top corner close to the painted black curve of the smokebox. However on No 60001 *Sir Ronald Matthews* and No 60002 *Andrew K. McCosh* the nameplates were located much further back on the side of the boiler casing with a very noticeable gap between the plate and the smokebox. There were variations with a number of the 'A4' class as to the positioning of the nameplates.

The nameplates fitted to No 60014 *Silver Link* and No 60015 *Quicksilver* had rounded corners whilst those fitted to the rest of the class had square corners and although cast in brass were originally chrome plated.

NAME CHANGES AND REPLACEMENT PLATES

A number of the 'A4s' were renamed, the majority of these losing the 'fast birds' names, which were replaced by names of directors of the LNER.

Above:
No 4482 Golden Eagle in LNER green livery which was only carried by 'A4s' for one year. (CR/GF)

Left above:
No 2509 Silver Link in original grey and silver livery for the 'Silver Jubilee' train in 1935. The name at first was painted on the side of the boiler casing. The locomotive is on the up 'Flying Scotsman' service at Grantham station, June 1937. (CR/JAW)

Far left:
A close up of the LNER transfers (gold shaded with red) on the tender of No 4500 Garganey (later named Sir Ronald Matthews). (CR/HML)

LIVERY TABLE

This uses the BR final number and name as the primary reference.

BR No	Name	Silver Grey	Green	Garter Blue LNER	Black LNER	Black NE	Garter Blue (red/white) lining	BR Blue/ Purple	Dark Blue Black and White Lining	BR Brunswick Green
60001	Sir Ronald Matthews			26/04/38	07/12/41	10/43	11/46		10/02/50	02/08/51
60002	Sir Murrough Wilson			12/04/38	07/02/42	11/03/43	11/10/46		02/02/50	14/08/51
60003	Andrew K. McCosh		12/08/37	20/10/38		21/08/42	21/06/47		19/04/50	10/10/51
60004	William Whitelaw			10/12/37		31/10/42	14/11/46		10/08/50	29/02/52
60005	Sir Charles Newton			08/08/38		22/08/42	28/01/48		23/11/49	11/11/52
60006	Sir Ralph Wedgwood			26/01/38	13/02/42	06/01/44	02/04/47		31/05/50	17/10/51
60007	Sir Nigel Gresley			30/10/37	21/02/42	20/10/43	06/03/47		27/09/50	17/04/52
60008	Dwight D. Eisenhower			04/09/37	30/01/42	12/03/43	25/09/45		14/06/50	09/11/51
60009	Union of South Africa			19/04/37	21/03/42	14/08/43	21/02/47		04/08/49	02/10/52
60010	Dominion of Canada			24/05/37	21/02/42	27/11/43	20/11/47		29/09/50	08/05/52
60011	Empire of India			15/05/37		22/10/42	30/11/46		08/06/50	10/04/52
60012	Commonwealth of Australia			15/05/37		12/09/42	09/08/47		24/08/49	21/11/52
60013	Dominion of New Zealand			27/06/37	21/11/41	20/11/43	17/08/46		20/05/49	08/10/52
60014	Silver Link	07/09/35		06/12/37	06/12/41	10/02/44	14/06/46		22/06/49	04/01/52
60015	Quicksilver	21/09/35		28/05/28		05/10/43	04/10/47		25/11/49	22/11/51
60016	Silver King	05/11/35		09/08/38		10/04/43	10/05/47		21/10/49	10/07/52
60017	Silver Fox	18/12/35		06/11/37	22/11/41	05/08/43	25/09/47		21/09/50	21/12/52
60018	Sparrow Hawk			27/11/37		22/08/43	28/12/46		05/04/50	04/10/51
60019	Bittern			18/12/37	14/11/41	22/05/43	07/03/47		28/07/50	12/02/52
60020	Guillemot			08/01/38		07/08/43	26/10/46		28/04/50	30/11/51
60021	Wild Swan			19/02/38	11/04/42	05/02/44	30/04/37		31/03/50	08/08/51
60022	Mallard			03/03/38	13/06/42	21/10/43	05/03/48		16/09/49	04/07/52
60023	Golden Eagle		22/12/36	29/01/38		10/09/43	28/09/46		31/08/49	04/09/52
60024	Kingfisher		26/12/36	07/01/38		04/02/43	31/08/46	18/06/48	24/08/50	12/03/52
60025	Falcon		23/01/37	18/12/37	30/11/41	21/07/43	31/12/47		27/01/50	06/12/52
60026	Miles Beevor		20/02/37	08/12/37	18/01/42	12/09/43	01/11/47		23/09/49	24/10/52
60027	Merlin		13/03/37	18/12/37	27/12/41	17/06/43	25/01/47	02/06/48	07/07/50	06/06/52
60028	Walter K. Whigham		20/03/37	12/02/38	22/11/41	30/01/44	01/10/47	07/06/48	13/10/50	22/02/52
60029	Woodcock		26/07/37	25/07/38		11/09/42	04/06/47	16/07/48	13/01/50	30/10/52
60030	Golden Fleece		30/08/37	25/09/37	20/12/41	22/11/42	07/12/46`		10/11/49	24/09/52
60031	Golden Plover			02/10/37	16/05/42	05/12/42	01/08/47		05/07/49	23/07/52
60032	Gannet			17/05/38		04/09/42	03/05/47		10/06/49	24/10/52
60033	Seagull			28/06/38	27/05/42	24/09/43	05/12/47		10/11/50	13/06/52
60034	Lord Faringdon			01/07/38		14/09/42	10/12/47		04/12/50	07/08/52

Above:
No 60024 Kingfisher painted in the short-lived BR Purple. This was only carried by four locomotives between 1948/50. (AC)

No 60004 *Great Snipe* had the distinction of being used on two different locomotives but neither of which was named after an LNER director. Some of the 'bird' series names would have been obscure to anyone not interested in ornithology and the replacement names with a title such as Lord or Sir bestowed a distinguished note.

At the time No 60008 *Golden Shuttle* (as No 4496) was re-named *Dwight D. Eisenhower* there was a proposal to re-name No 60029 *Woodcock* (as No 4493) *Montgomery* but this was not carried out.

An announcement in 1947 proposed that No 60011 *Empire of India* should be re-named

Number	Name	Original Name	Date of Change
No 60001	Sir Ronald Matthews	Garganey	March 1939
No 60002	Sir Murrough Wilson	Pochard	April 1939
No 60003	Andrew K. McCosh	Osprey	August 1942
No 60004	William Whitelaw	Great Snipe	July 1941
No 60005	Sir Charles Newton	Capercaillie	August 1942
No 60006	Sir Ralph Wedgwood	Herring Gull	January 1944
No 60008	Dwight D. Eisenhower	Golden Shuttle	September 1945 (covered until 02/1946)
No 60010	Dominion of Canada	Woodcock	June 1937
No 60026	Miles Beevor	Kestrel	November 1947
No 60028	Walter K. Whigham	Sea Eagle	October 1947
No 60030	Golden Fleece	Great Snipe	July 1937 (Great Snipe re-used on 60004)
No 60034	Lord Faringdon	Peregrine	March 1948
No 4469	Sir Ralph Wedgwood	Gadwall	March 1939

Above:
The cast stainless steel fox mounted on the boiler casing of No 60017 Silver Fox. It remained in position for the working life of the locomotive. (GM)

Right:
The plaque fitted to the boiler casing of No 60022 Mallard to commemorate the world speed record in 1938 was not carried until 1948. (GM)

Dominion of India and new name plates were fitted whilst in Doncaster works, but the Empire of India plates were re-fitted when the locomotive was put back into traffic. The same announcement also proposed that No 60020 (No 4465) Guillemot should be re-named Dominion of Pakistan but this was not carried out. Also No 60010 (as No 4489) Woodcock was to have been re-named Buzzard but this was never happened.

RED-PAINTED NAMEPLATES

The usual colour for the background of the 'A4' class nameplates was black. However in 1938 the following locomotives were observed carrying nameplates with a light red background: Silver Link, Quicksilver, Silver King, Silver Fox, Union of South Africa, Woodcock, Empire of India, Commonwealth of Australia, Dominion of New Zealand, Great Snipe and Golden Shuttle. In 1939 Sir Ralph Wedgwood, Sir Nigel Gresley, Sir Murrough Wilson and Sir Ronald Matthews received plates with a light red background and also stainless steel embellishments.

In BR days staff at King's Cross shed, for a short period, painted the nameplate background red until there was a complaint and the background colour reverted to black. Some of the Scottish region locomotives also had red background nameplates following transfer to the north.

The following list identified from photographs shows some of the locomotives so fitted and date. The list is not exhaustive and there could be other examples.

Locomotive	Date(s)
No 60007 Sir Nigel Gresley	Circa 1963
No 60008 Dwight D. Eisenhower	Circa 1958
No 60010 Silver Link	Circa 1961
No 60015 Quicksilver	
No 60017 Silver Fox	Circa 1958 and 1963
No 60019 Bittern	Circa 1966
No 60022 Mallard	Circa 1960
No 60024 Kingfisher	Circa 1966
No 60025 Falcon	Circa 1961, by 1962 black
No 60032 Gannet	
No 60034 Lord Faringdon	Circa 1966

BLUE-PAINTED NAMEPLATES

In BR days two locomotives, No 60011 Empire of India and No 60004 William Whitelaw, had nameplates with a pale blue background. This colour was used by all Scottish sheds and was similar to the colour used on station totems in Scotland. This colour was also seen on a small number of 'A1s' as well as on the smokebox number plates of a range of locomotive classes.

Above:
An example of the painted name as on the first four locomotives, the lettering is yellow shaded with dark blue. (IA)

YELLOW STRIPE ON CAB SIDE

Below:
No 60031 Golden
Plover at Perth,
August 1965. The
yellow warning stripe
through the cabside
number had been
applied in error. (CR)

Two 'A4s' (No 60027 *Merlin* and No 60031 *Golden Plover*) had a yellow warning stripe applied (August 1964) to the cab side which was intended to warn crews that the locomotive was not authorised to work south of Crewe on the West Coast route to Euston. It was thought that the overhead power wires would come close to the top of the locomotive with the possible risk of electrical arcing. The chances of these two 'A4s' working south of Crewe was somewhat remote. At the time the two locomotives were allocated to ex-LMS depots and the instruction to apply the stripe had been sent to all depots in that region irrespective of location.

Interestingly the 'A4s' were not listed on the official list detailing which classes should have the stripe so it was simply a mistake for it to have been applied. Both locomotives were originally allocated to St Rollox: No 60027 between May 1962 and September 1964; No 60031 between February 1962 and October 1965.

PLAQUES & EMBELLISHMENTS

A number of locomotives were fitted with embelishments as follows:

No 60007 *Sir Nigel Gresley*. Along with the five locomotives built for the 'Coronation' service, it was fitted with a stainless strip along the edge of the valance skirting and the tender edge when first built. This was subsequently removed from the locomotive.

No 60009 *Union of South Africa*. A plaque in the form of a springbok was fitted in 1954 to the left-hand side of the locomotive having been donated by a Bloemfontein newspaper proprietor. It is not clear why only one plaque was made. The springbok was originally located on the side of the boiler casing but in preservation it has been moved to the cab side.

No 60010 *Dominion of Canada*. As No 4489 it was fitted with a Canadian Pacific Railway Company (CPR) bell in front of the chimney on 11 March 1938. When the locomotive was fitted with a double chimney on 27 December 1957 the bell was removed.

The five locomotives built for the 'Coronation' service had the coat of arms of the respective countries on the cab sides. These were painted by hand at Doncaster works onto metal plates which were then screwed to the cab sides (displacing the works plates, see note later). No 60009 *Union of*

South Africa and No 60011 *Empire of India* retained the plaques until withdrawal from service in 1966 and 1964 respectively. These locomotives were also fitted with a stainless steel strip along the valance skirting and on the edge of the tender footplate when first built. The strip on the locomotive was subsequently removed but remained on the tenders. This was subsequently painted over but can be clearly seen on the appropriate tenders up to withdrawal.

No 60017 *Silver Fox*. Two stainless steel leaping foxes were provided in 1935 by steelmakers Samuel Fox & Company Limited and fitted to the locomotive from new on each side of the boiler casing. The boiler bands of the locomotive when it was painted in grey were also stainless steel. A proposal was made to have a stainless boiler casing but this was never carried through.

No 60022 *Mallard*. Following the record breaking run a plaque commemorating the event was mounted, in 1948, at the centre of the boiler casing on both sides.

No 60024 *Kingfisher*. The captain and crew of HMS *Kingfisher* presented the locomotive with two plaques of a Kingfisher painted in full colour on copper. These were presented by the maker Lieutenant A. Mortimer RN, and were fitted in May 1946 (at Haymarket shed) to the cab sides. From June 1948 the p.58 ▶

Above:
A close up of the CPR-type bell fitted to No 4489 Dominion of Canada in 1938 and removed in 1957 when it was fitted with a double chimney.

Above left:
No 4489 Dominion of Canada in full 'Coronation' livery of Garter Blue and red wheels. Note the coat of arms on the cab. (IA)

Right:
No 60028 Walter K. Whigham in the short-lived BR Purple livery. The lining on the valance edge continues round the end to near the buffers. Note the works plate usually fitted below the numbers has been moved to inside the cab. (CR/JJ)

Left:
No 60032 Gannet finished in dark blue with black and white lining. Note the first version of the BR totem on the tender. The locomotive is ex-works Doncaster in June 1949. (CR/HML)

No 4487 Sea Eagle in 1937 finished in LNER Green, but with the black of the smokebox painted as far back as the first boiler casing band. This livery was only applied to Kingfisher, Falcon, Kestrel, Merlin and Sea Eagle. The livery lasted approximately 12 months when all the locomotives were re-painted Garter Blue. This was between December 1937 and February 1938. (D. W. Allen)

Above:
No 60033 Seagull in the post-war version of the LNER Garter Blue. (CR/JFA)

Right above:
No 60005 Sir Charles Newton in BR Blue livery lined in black and white. Note the shed name painted on the front. (CR/TO)

Right:
No 60022 Mallard leaving Edinburgh (Waverley) with the southbound 'The Elizabethan' in September 1961. The locomotive is finished in the final BR livery with the second version of the BR totem on the tender. Note the overhead power warning flashes. (CR/JBS)

No 60019 Bittern at St. Rollox, 3 September 1966, its last day in service. Note the firebox boiler band is lined out. (J. R. Carter)

plaques were moved to the side of the boiler casing. A photograph taken of the locomotive being shunted into Hughes of Blyth yard for scrapping in November 1966 shows what appears to be at least one of the plaques still in place (this may have been the backing plate).

No 60027 *Merlin*. The captain and personnel of HMS *Merlin* (an Admiralty shore establishment) presented a set of plaques in 1946 which were originally fixed on the cab sides (requiring the works plates to be moved to the inside of the cab). The plaques were subsequently moved to the sides of the boiler casing. The plaques depicted the badge of HMS *Merlin*. The reason for the plaques was that the establishment was 'adopted' by the City of Edinburgh and No 60027 *Merlin* was a long-term resident of Haymarket shed.

SHED NAME

At various times after 1948 in addition to the shed plate bolted below the smokebox door the shed name was sometimes painted above the right-hand (looking from the front) buffer.

Examples and dates are given below. Notice that Gateshead (G'Head) and King's Cross (King's +) had two forms, one in full and one abbreviated.

Number	Name	Shed Name	Date(s)
No 60003	Andrew K. McCosh	King's +	Circa 1950s
No 60004	William Whitelaw	Haymarket	Circa 1949
No 60005	Sir Charles Newton	Gateshead	Circa 1950
No 60011	Empire of India	Haymarket	Circa 1948/49
No 60014	Silver Link	King's +	1950
No 60016	Silver King	G'Head	Summer 1949
No 60018	Sparrow Hawk	Gateshead	August 1949
No 60019	Bittern	Ferryhill	Circa 1960s
No 60019	Bittern	Gateshead	August 1949
No 60022	Mallard	King's +	
No 60026	Miles Beevor	Grantham	Pre 1957
No 60027	Merlin	Haymarket	Circa 1948/49
No 60029	Woodcock	King's Cross	Circa 1949
No 60030	Golden Fleece	Grantham	Circa 1950
No 60031	Golden Plover	Haymarket	Circa 1949/50
No 60033	Seagull	King's +	Circa 1948/49

Below:
No 60027 Merlin at King's Cross, 20 August 1960. Note the plaque of HMS Merlin has been moved from the cab side to the boiler casing (RAS)

WORKS PLATES

The normal position for the two works plates was below the number on the cab sides but this was not standard throughout the class.

The batch built in 1937 and named after the Dominions (and used on the 'Coronation' service) had the coat of arms of that country below the number on the cab side leaving no room for the works plate. This was then fitted inside the cab. The works plates were retained in this position long after the coat of arms had been removed.

Other locomotives also ran with works plates inside the cab:

No 60026 *Miles Beevor*
No 60028 *Walter K. Whigham*
The plates on both were moved to inside the cab when the locomotives were renamed in 1947.

No 60027 *Merlin* had the works plates moved inside the cab when the plaques were originally fitted to the cab sides in 1946. When the plaques were moved to the boiler casing the works plates remained inside the cab.

No 60007 *Sir Nigel Gresley* also had a replacement set of works plates seen in the 1960s which were of a different style to that previously fitted (the replacement being of the style found on Darlington built 'A1s').

Above:
No 60024 Kingfisher in the final BR livery. It has red background nameplates and is fitted with a non-corridor tender. Note the mounting plate for the Kingfisher plaque (not fitted). The locomotive is on the St Margaret's turntable, September 1966. (CR/GMS)

Right:
No 60031 Golden
Plover waiting to
back down to King's
Cross. It is finished in
BR green livery, but
without overhead
warning flashes.
On the totem the lion
is facing the wrong
way; it should always
face to the left. This
was a common
mistake in all the
BR workshops.
(Eric Treacy)

SMOKEBOX NUMBER PLATE

The 'A4s' shared with the 'A3' Pacifics on the Eastern Region two different styles to the numeral 6 (and 9); one a 'straight' 6 (the correct BR Gill Sans style) and one where the top curls over. The curly 6 was usually fitted when the BR numbers were originally used (and appears to have been the LNER's interpretation of the BR-style numeral) but when replacement plates were subsequently fitted these tended to be the correct Gill Sans 'straight' 6. Replacement smokebox plates were being made as late as 1963.

If there was a numeral 9 in the number this would be in the same style as the numeral 6.

From photographs the following locomotives were fitted with the 'straight' numeral 6 (there may have been others and the dates are only approximate):

No 60004:	curly 1948/1953, straight 1965
No 60005:	1951/52, 1960
No 60006:	1950-1962
No 60008:	1957/58, 1961
No 60009:	curly 1960/61 straight 1964/65
No 60011:	curly 1952, straight 1962/63
No 60013:	1955, 1958, 1963
No 60014:	1954-1961
No 60016:	1953-1963
No 60017:	1957, 1963
No 60019:	1962/65
No 60023:	curly 1960, straight 1963
No 60025:	1953-1961
No 60026:	1950-1961
No 60028:	curly 1959, straight 1961/62
No 60031:	curly in 1949, straight 1959-1961
No 60032:	1951-1961
No 60033:	1961/62
No 60034:	curly up to 1963, straight from February 1963 (replacement plate fitted)

CHAPTER SIX

IN SERVICE

The 'A4' class was only ever allocated to a small number of sheds, the primary being King's Cross (London), Gateshead (Newcastle) and Haymarket (Edinburgh).

Class A4 locomotives were used to haul the most important trains on the LNER (and later the Eastern Region of BR) and were in service until the end of steam. Even in those last days 'A4s' were selected for the accelerated service between Glasgow and Aberdeen.

ROUTES

The *raison d'être* of the class was to haul express passenger trains on the East Coast main line from King's Cross to Newcastle and Edinburgh, in some cases non-stop. Over the years a number of services became associated with the 'A4s' such as 'The Silver Jubilee' (Newcastle – London), Coronation (London-Edinburgh) and 'The Flying Scotsman'. A number were also specifically built to work express trains to and from Leeds ('The West Riding Limited', 'The Yorkshire Pullman'). Locomotives even had names such as *Golden Fleece* and *Golden Shuttle* to associate with the Yorkshire wool trade. In BR days trains such as 'The Fair Maid', a Perth to London service which ran non-stop on the leg between Newcastle and London, and 'The Elizabethan' (re-named from 'The Capitals Limited') this was again a non-stop London-Edinburgh service as was 'The Talisman'.

Only after the reallocation to the Glasgow (Buchanan Street)-Aberdeen route in 1963 did 'A4s' regularly work services to these cities.

The 'A4' class was rarely used away from these routes and examples of 'wandering' are listed in the section Foreign Travels.

ALLOCATIONS

The locomotives were only ever allocated to a small number of sheds, the primary being King's Cross, Gateshead (Newcastle) and Haymarket (Edinburgh).

During World War Two, Gateshead locomotives were also allocated at Heaton on the east side of Newcastle and King's Cross locomotives to Grantham, Lincolnshire. In both cases this was presumably to alleviate staffing shortages. This also applied after 1945 when King's Cross locomotives were moved to Grantham again. When King's Cross shed closed in 1963 all 'A4s' were moved to Peterborough (New England shed). The re-location to Scotland of some of this group meant sheds such as Aberdeen, St Rollox and St Margaret's acquired 'A4s' for the first time. The locomotives allocated to Dalry Road, Glasgow were actually placed in store there and then moved on to sheds such as Aberdeen to be re-instated to traffic.

Before World War Two for short periods a small number of 'A4s' were also allocated to Doncaster.

No 60001 *Sir Ronald Matthews* was allocated to Gateshead shed for the locomotive's p.69 ▶

Above:
No 4489 Dominion of Canada in full blue livery with stainless-steel letters and numbers. It is departing King's Cross with an up express in mid-1939. (CR/HML)

Left:
The driver of No 60003 Andrew K. McCosh watches the way ahead as the locomotive departs Leeds Central with an express to King's Cross in the 1960s. The letters RA9 (lower right corner of the cab side) refer to the locomotive's route availability. (Eric Treacy)

Right:
No 60003 Andrew K. McCosh departs Leeds with an express, passing one of the recently introduced Class 55 'Deltic' diesels. Note the 'curly' number 6 on the plate fitted to the smokebox door plate. The BR-type speedometer drive is clearly visible fitted to the rear driving wheel on the driver's side. (Eric Treacy)

Right:
No 60002 Sir Murrough Wilson in typical Gateshead condition, and final BR condition, waits for duty in March 1964. It always had a non-corridor tender as it was at Gateshead for its entire life. (CR)

Left:
No 60011 Empire of India at Newcastle Central with the down 'Flying Scotsman' in August 1947. It is finished in post-war Garter Blue livery complete with 'LNER' on the tender. Note the red-backed nameplate and the long cylinder drain pipes clipped to the front guard irons. (CR/HJ)

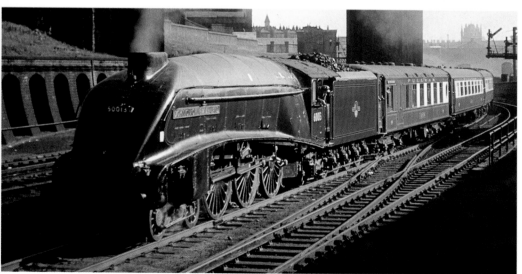

Left:
No 60013 Dominion of New Zealand on the approaches to King's Cross is in final BR condition, September 1961. Note the non-standard whistle fitted to this locomotive. (CR/ACS)

Above:
No 4462 Great Snipe at Grantham with a down express in the 1930s. (RAS)

Right:
No 60027 Merlin leaves Dundee with an Edinburgh train in July 1965. This was one of two 'A4s' which had yellow stripes incorrectly applied in 1964. The crest once fitted to this locomotive is missing.
(D. Mackinnon)

Above:
No 4466 Herring Gull
at Retford in 1938
on an express. The
locomotive is in blue
with gold and red
transfers. (RAS)

entire service life. No 60018 *Sparrow Hawk* and No 60020 *Guillemot* were also allocated to Gateshead shed for service (except for a short stay at Heaton during World War Two).

FOREIGN TRAVELS

The 'A4s' were only used to work away from 'home territory' as a result of running on special trains, and the following are some examples of these workings far removed from the East Coast main line. Also including are the rare occasions when 'A4s' worked 'regular' trains away from home.

No 60007 *Sir Nigel Gresley*. In 1938 ran an LNER exhibition train from and to Manchester Exchange via the Woodhead route.

No 60007 *Sir Nigel Gresley*. A rail tour from Manchester to Marylebone, London via Crewe, Shrewsbury–Wolverhampton–Birmingham (Snow Hill) and Marylebone in 1965.

No 60011 *Empire of India*. Worked the up 'Waverley' (due to the failure of the booked diesel) between Edinburgh and Leeds via the Waverley route, and the Settle and Carlisle line on 25 March 1962. Locomotive serviced at Leeds Holbeck shed.

No 60014 *Silver Link*. Ian Allan special 'Pennine Pullman' worked north from Marylebone, London with this train to Sheffield on 12 June 1956.

No 60022 *Mallard*. Exchange Trials 1948, used on the Southern Region between Waterloo, London and Exeter, Devon.

A Locomotive Club of Great Britain (LCGB) special from Waterloo, London to Exeter, Devon on 24 February 1963.

No 60021 *Wild Swan*. Worked through to Derby (via Sheffield) with the 12.19 Newcastle-Bristol train on 9 October 1963.

No 60023 *Golden Eagle*. Railway Correspondents Travel Society (RCTS) special Hellifield, nr Skipton-Carlisle-Tebay-Hellifield in 1963.

No 60024 *Kingfisher*. An LCGB rail tour from Waterloo, London to Weymouth, Dorset in March 1968.

No 60030 *Golden Fleece*. In the 1940s (when running as No 4495) seen as a light locomotive on the Woodhead route; the reason is unknown.

No 60033 *Seagull*. Exchange Trials 1948, on the Western Region between Paddington, London and Plymouth, Devon. Also on the Southern Region between Waterloo, London and Exeter, Devon.

Above:
'A4s' meet at Peterborough. No 60010 Dominion of Canada on an up express meets No 60013 Dominion of New Zealand with a down Scotch Goods, June 1962. (CR/DWW)

Above left:
Gateshead shed's No 60018 Sparrow Hawk on an express in August 1961. This locomotive was one of the least photgraphed 'A4s'. (CR/NFI)

Left:
No 60031 Golden Plover on 'The Elizabethan' at Newcastle, June 1968. Note the red-backed nameplate and Haymarket shed plate. (CR/RSH)

Far left:
No 60022 Mallard in final BR condition in 1962 with overhead power warning flashes. Note the 'curly' six on the smokebox number plate. (CR/CBC)

Above:
No 60011 Empire of India at Holbeck shed Leeds having worked in from Edinburgh via Carlisle. Note the blue background to the nameplate. (GM)

Right:
No 60014 Silver Link at Helpston crossing with 'The Elizabethan' down service in 1961. (D. C. Ovenden)

No 60034 *Lord Faringdon*. Exchange Trials 1948, on the London Midland region between Euston, London and Carlisle.

REPAIR LOCATIONS

The Works primarily responsible for the repair of the 'A4' class was Doncaster and the last to receive repairs there was No 60009 *Union of South Africa* in November 1963. Other workshops also carried out repairs:

Darlington. With the ending of steam repairs at Doncaster at the end of 1963, Darlington took over the primary responsibility for repairs and the following locomotives are recorded as having visited the works.

    No 60004: February 1964, August 1965
    No 60009: April 1964
    No 60010: May 1965 (not repaired)
    No 60011: April 1964 (not repaired, scrapped)
    No 60019: March 1965 (heavy/intermediate)
    No 60020: March 1964 (for cutting up)
    No 60024: September 1964 (heavy/intermediate), July 1965 (casual/light)
    No 60026: May 1965
    No 60034: April 1965 (heavy/intermediate)

Inverurie (Aberdeen). As this was considerably closer than Darlington to the sheds at Aberdeen and St Rollox (to which the locomotives were allocated) light casual repairs or non-classified repairs were carried out on the following 'A4s':

    No 60004: February 1964, May 1965
    No 60006: March 1965
    No 60007: December 1964, April 1965
    No 60012: September 1963, February 1964
    No 60019: May 1965
    No 60026: May 1965

Cowlairs (Glasgow). Again considerably closer than Darlington, light casual or non-classified repairs were carried out on the following:

    No 60019: April 1966
    No 60031: September 1964, August 1965

Haymarket Shed. No 60009 is listed as having a non-classified repair in December 1963.

Stratford Works. No 60034 visited Stratford in 1954 for repairs to the tender.

WITHDRAWALS

The first 'A4' withdrawn following bomb damage at York shed was No 4469 *Gadwall* in 1942. It is surprising that a replacement was not built but by now Edward Thompson was the LNER's Chief Mechanical Engineer (CME) and is highly unlikely to have authorised the building of another Gresley locomotive and new build for a 'one-off' would have been difficult in the depths of wartime. By the time the war ended Thompson and subsequently Peppercorn 'A1' and 'A2' class Pacifics were the order of the day for new builds.

p.76 ▶

Above:
No 60001 Sir Ronald Matthews passes North Queensferry with a cattle train from Aberdeen in 1952. (RAS)

Above:
No 60013 Dominion of New Zealand in August 1958 prior to the fitting of a BR-type speedometer. (CR/DBS)

Right:
No 60025 Falcon on an express in its final condition, leaving Leeds Central in 1961. (GM)

Above:
No 60021 Wild Swan with red-painted nameplate and single chimney in May 1957. (CR/EVF)

Left:
The down Scotch Goods hauled by an immaculate No 60017 Silver Fox in April 1963 near the end of steam services on the southern end of the Eastern region. (RAS/KLC)

Right:
No 4495 Golden
Fleece and Golden
Shuttle both in blue
livery. Golden Fleece
is fitted with
stainless-steel
numbers and
lettering. (IA)

Following the introduction of the English Electric Type 4 (Class 40) diesel in 1959 the 'A3s' were seldom used for top linkwork. The death blow to the 'A4' class was the introduction of the English Electric Type 5 (Class 55) 'Deltics' starting in 1961 (and completed by 1962) leading to the first of the 'A4' class to be withdrawn at the end of 1962. The locomotives were No 60003 *Andrew K.*

McCosh, No 60014 *Silver Link*, No 60028 *Walter K. Wigham*, No 60030 *Golden Fleece* and No 60033 *Seagull* in December 1962. With the imminent closure of King's Cross shed in June 1963, No 60013 *Dominion of New Zealand*, No 60015 *Quicksilver* and No 60022 *Mallard* were withdrawn (April 1963) and the remaining 'A4s' at King's Cross transferred to Peterborough (New

76

England). Here they lasted a few months before the ending of steam services at the southern end of the East Coast main line. This resulted in a further 'culling' of 'A4s' with the withdrawal of No 60008 *Dwight D. Eisenhower* (July 1963), No 60017 *Silver Fox* (October 1963), No 60021 *Wild Swan* (October 1963), No 60025 *Falcon* (October 1963) and No 60032 *Gannet* (October 1963).

The remaining 'A4s' at New England (No 60006 *Sir Ralph Wedgwood*, No 60007 *Sir Nigel Gresley*, No 60010 *Dominion of Canada* and No 60026 *Miles Beevor*) were then transferred to Scotland to work the three-hour service to Aberdeen, and joined the four locomotives transferred from Gateshead and the remaining 'A4s' on the Scottish region.

The 'A4s' allocated to Gateshead lasted a little longer than those at New England but were soon withdrawn in 1963 and 1964: No 60018 *Sparrow Hawk* in June 1963, No 60020 *Guillemot* in March 1964 and No 60002 *Sir Murrough Wilson* in May 1964. The four Gateshead locomotives were moved north to Scotland to work the Aberdeen trains.

The surviving group in Scotland were gradually withdrawn during 1965 and 1966, this being dictated generally by condition, any major fault usually leading to the scrapping of the locomotive.

The last two survivors were No 60019 *Bittern* and No 60024 *Kingfisher* but both were withdrawn in September 1966. *Kingfisher* worked the last regular passenger train hauled by an 'A4' on 14 September 1966 on the 8.45 am Glasgow (Buchanan Street) to Aberdeen.

No 60019 *Bittern* arrived (in preservation) at York in full-working condition and was almost immediately used working special trains when preserved, as did No 60007 *Sir Nigel Gresley*, that is until BR banned mainline steam working completely towards the end of 1967. Both locomotives were then sold to private owners.

DISPOSALS

The 'A4s' withdrawn before the end of 1963 were all scrapped at Doncaster; the last 'A4' cut up there was No 60025 *Falcon* in January 1964. In the early years of scrapping some parts were re-used for other locomotives in the class. A photograph of No 60014 *Silver Link* being cut up at Doncaster, in early 1963, shows a chalked message 'keep bogie' and presumably this (or parts such as bogie wheels) was re-used on any 'A4s' receiving attention at Doncaster up to the end of the year when steam repairs ceased.

Subsequent to that date some 'A4s' were cut up at Darlington and some were sold to private scrap yards.

In the later years of the class a number were sent to Darlington for overhaul but when stripped were found to be in poor condition and were subsequently condemned. As an example No 60010 *Dominion of Canada* arrived at Darlington in steam for repair from Aberdeen (Ferryhill) but the boiler was found to be in a very poor state and the locomotive was condemned. No 60026 *Miles Beevor* was the last 'A4' to be scrapped in August 1967 despite

Left:
No 60030 Golden
Fleece on a down
Scotch Goods in
1962. This was one
of most important
workings to and
from King's Cross
goods yard and
often entrusted to
an 'A4'. (RAS/KLC)

Below:
No 60009 Union of
South Africa on one
of the three-hour
expresses between
Glasgow and
Aberdeen. (GM)

Right:
No 60006 Sir Ralph Wedgwood on a fast freight in 1962. (AC)

Below:
No 2512 Silver Fox working 'The Silver Jubilee' service with special coaching stock. (AC)

having been withdrawn in August 1965. The locomotive was stored at three different locations and then sent to Crewe to provide spare parts (including driving wheels) for No 60007 *Sir Nigel Gresley* which at the time was being overhauled at Crewe. No 60026 *Miles Beevor* was condemned at Perth and then sold to Motherwell Machinery & Scrap Company and delivered to Motherwell but the sale was cancelled and the locomotive returned to Perth for storage.

The following lists the sites where 'A4s' were scrapped and also indicates any details of storage (where known), before scrapping.

DONCASTER WORKS: No 60003 *Andrew K. McCosh*, No 60013 *Dominion of New Zealand*, No 60014 *Silver Link*, No 60015 *Quicksilver*, No 60017 *Silver Fox*, No 60018 *Sparrow Hawk*, No 60021 *Wild Swan*, No 60025 *Falcon*, No 60028 *Walter K. Whigham*, No 60029 *Woodcock*, No 60030 *Golden Fleece*, No 60032 *Gannet*, and No 60033 *Seagull*.

DARLINGTON WORKS: No 60011 *Empire of India*, and No 60020 *Guillemot* (March 1964).

THE MOTHERWELL MACHINERY & SCRAP COMPANY, Wishaw, Nr Glasgow: No 60004 *William Whitelaw*, No 60006 *Sir Ralph Wedgwood*, No 60012 *Commonwealth of Australia*, No 60016 *Silver King* and No 60023 *Golden Eagle*.

HUGHES OF BLYTH, Nr Newcastle: No 60001 *Sir Ronald Matthews* (after storage at Heaton, scrapped January 1965), No 60024 *Kingfisher* (from Aberdeen, November 1966), No 60026 *Miles Beevor* (August 1967) and No 60034 *Lord Faringdon* (from Perth, November 1966).

GEORGE H. CAMBELL, Shieldhill, Nr Falkirk: No 60027 *Merlin*, and No 60031 *Golden Plover* (both early 1966).

GEORGE H. CAMBELL, Airdrie, Nr Glasgow: No 60005 *Sir Charles Newton*.

GEORGE COHEN LIMITED, Cargo Fleet, Middlesbrough: No 60002 *Sir Murrough Wilson* (after storage at Heaton, scrapped in October 1964).

Right:
No 60006 Dominion of New Zealand works the down Scotch Goods in June 1962. This working was considered to be as important as any express passenger train and often entrusted to a King's Cross based 'A4'. (RAS)

Below:
No 60009 Union of South Africa is out-shopped as the last steam locomotive to be overhauled at Doncaster works, November 1963. (IA)

No 60034 Lord Faringdon leaves the Forth Bridge with an Edinburgh-Aberdeen fitted freight in 1964. (RAS)

CHAPTER SEVEN

PRESERVATION

A total of six Class A4 locomotives are in preservation,
and four have been used to operate steam 'specials'.
All are painted in either Garter Blue or Brunswick Green livery.

Withdrawals of the 'A4s' commenced in 1962, and if all the locomotives had remained on the Eastern region they would all have been withdrawn by 1964. However the transfer to Scotland extended the life of a number of locomotives by up to two years and thereby also assisted the preservation of Nos 60007, 60009, 60010 and 60019.

No 60007 *Sir Nigel Gresley*. Withdrawn in February 1966, it was purchased by the A4 Locomotive Society and moved to Crewe for overhaul, where No 60026 *Miles Beevor* was used for parts. These were in better condition than those on No 60007. Regrettably the hulk of No 60026 was sent to be scrapped. Following this major overhaul No 60007 ran regularly on the main line until BR's steam ban in late 1967. During the overhaul at Crewe the locomotive was painted in LNER Garter Blue livery (complete with red wheels, stainless steel lettering and numbers) but without valance panels. No 60007 remains in this livery. Since the steam ban was lifted in the 1970s *Sir Nigel Gresley* has been in regular use on main line 'specials'.

No 60008 *Dwight D. Eisenhower.* Withdrawn July 1963. Painted in Brunswick Green, it was presented by Dr (later Lord) Beeching on 27 April 1964 and shipped to the National Railway Museum, Green Bay, Wisconsin, USA.

No 60009 *Union of South Africa*. Withdrawn May 1966, remains painted in BR Brunswick Green livery and has been in regular use on main line 'specials' since entering preservation. The locomotive, based at the Severn Valley Railway, received a heavy overhaul in 2003. At the time of writing it is being prepared for main line running later in 2005.

No 60010 *Dominion of Canada*. Withdrawn May 1965, at Darlington works. Following a period of storage at Darlington shed (after the closure of Darlington works) the locomotive was moved to Crewe works where it was cosmetically restored in Brunswick Green and then shipped to Canada for display at the Canadian Railroad Historical Museum, near Montreal.

No 60019 *Bittern*. Withdrawn in September 1966 and like No 60007 immediately went into preservation. Based initially at York locomotive depot, it ran regularly on the main line until the BR steam ban in late 1967. At one point restored as *Silver Link* in grey livery (but not at that time in steaming condition) and is currently being re-built for use on the main line.

No 60022 *Mallard*. Resident at the National Railway Museum, York. It has been restored to 1938 condition with full skirting and valances. The locomotive was steamed in the 1980s but is unlikely to work again.

Above:
Sir Nigel Gresley
works a special
train near Blackburn
in the 1980s.
LNER Blue with
stainless steel
numbers and letters.
(AC)

Left:
No 60028 Walther K.
Whigham still fitted
with dust shields
modified to enable
an AWS contact to
be fitted. The front
number has the
'curly' six fitted,
rather than the
correct 'straight'.
(AC)

Left:
No 60024 Kingfisher, with the diamond-shape plaque fitted in the centre of the boiler casing. When presented the plaques were mounted on the side of the cab. (IA)

Far left:
The plaque depicting a Kingfisher was painted in full colour on a white background, the edge being left natural copper. It measured approximately 12.25in (311mm) high and 10in (254mm) wide. (IA)

Left:
The crest of HMS Merlin as fitted to No 60027 Merlin is approximately 14.5in (368mm) high and 11.5in (292mm) wide. The rope border, crown and name are gold on black. Background is a pale blue/green, white cliffs and blue sea and the bird is in black and grey. (IA)

Left:
No 60027 Merlin (with original LNER No 27) with the crest in the original position on the side of the cab, May 1946. The crests were moved in June 1948 to the centre of the boiler casing. (IA)

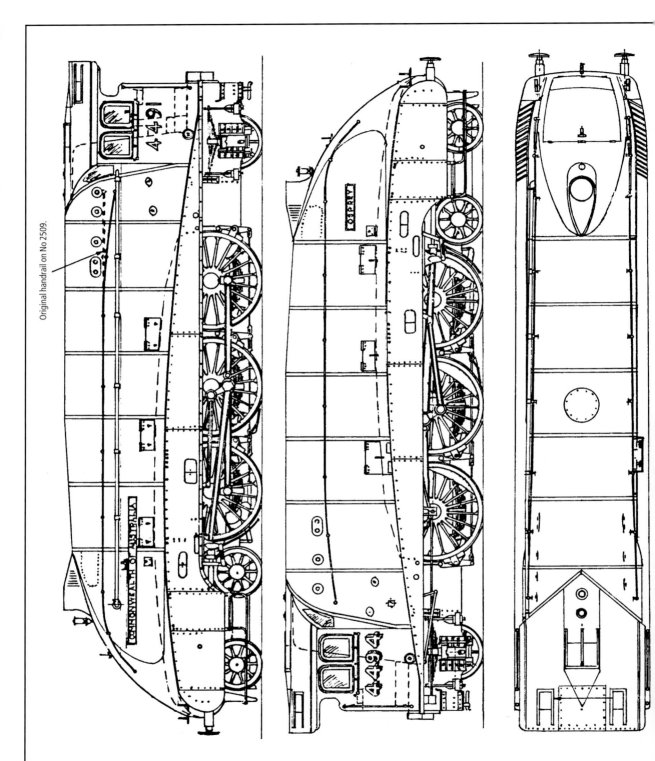

Original handrail on No 2509.

Gresley A4 LNER Streamlined Express

© Copyright 2005 Isinglass Drawings/John Edgson.

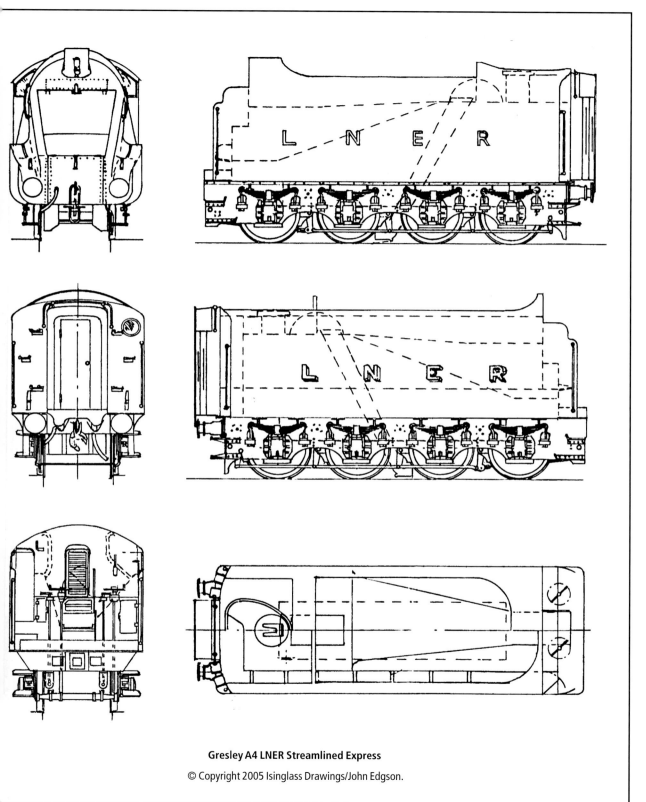

Gresley A4 LNER Streamlined Express

© Copyright 2005 Isinglass Drawings/John Edgson.

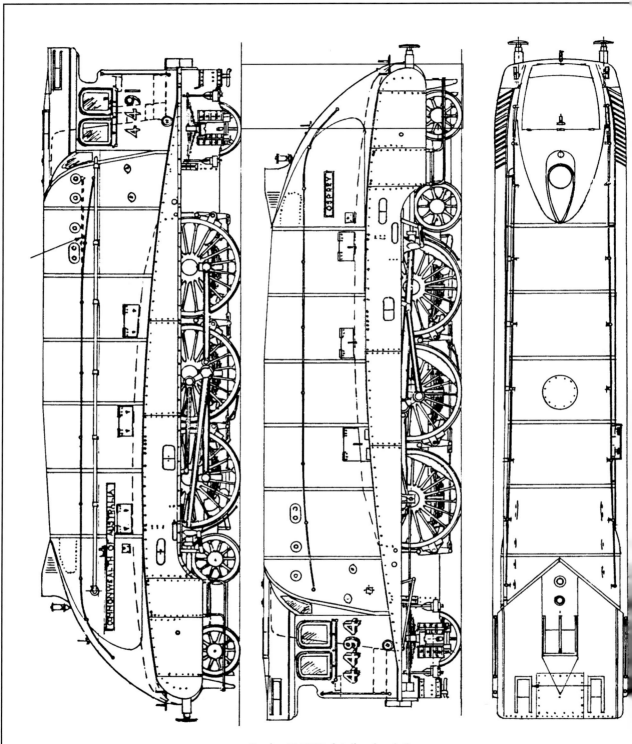

Gresley A4 LNER, detail and variation

© Copyright 2005 Isinglass Drawings/John Edgson.

Canadian whistle (5/37 to 4/49)
and bell (3/38 to 11/57) on No 4489.

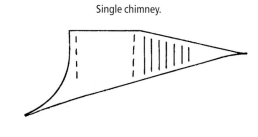

Single chimney.

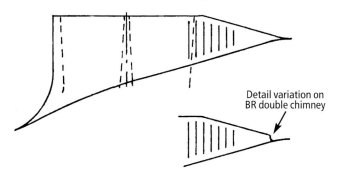

double chimney.

Detail variation on
BR double chimney

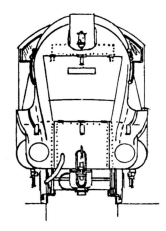

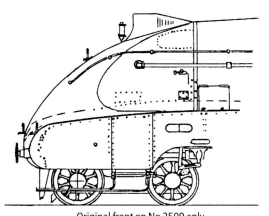

Original small access door
from April 1938.

Original front on No 2509 only.

Gresley A4 LNER, detail and variation

© Copyright 2005 Isinglass Drawings/John Edgson.

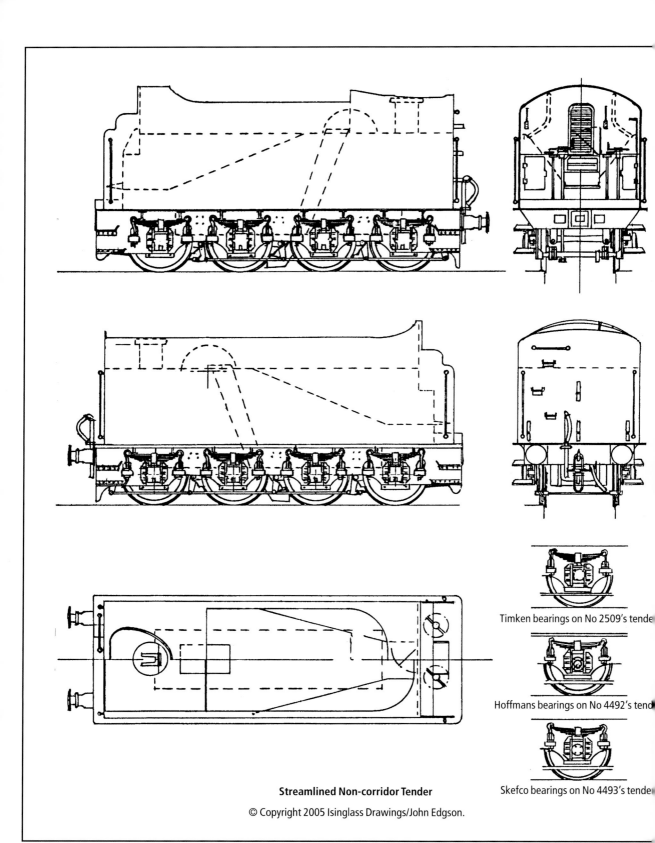

Timken bearings on No 2509's tender

Hoffmans bearings on No 4492's tender

Skefco bearings on No 4493's tender

Streamlined Non-corridor Tender

© Copyright 2005 Isinglass Drawings/John Edgson.

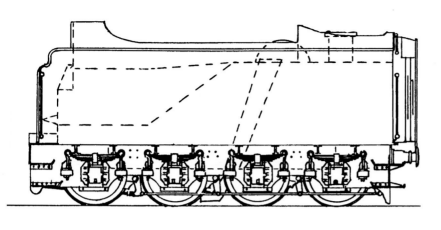
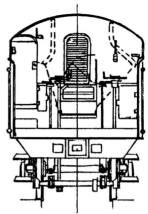
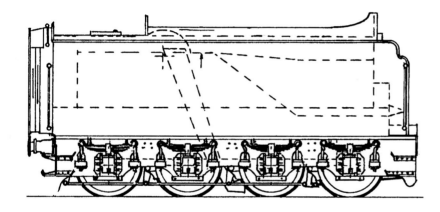
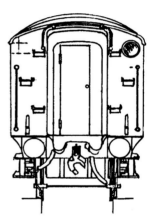
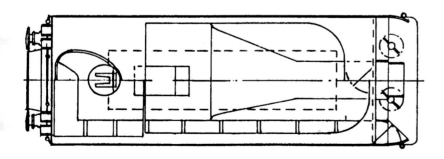

Modified ex A3 Corridor Tender

© Copyright 2005 Isinglass Drawings/John Edgson.

No 60001	G'Head			
No 60002	G'Head	King's +	August 1948	G'Head October 1943
No 60003	Heaton King's + May 1939	Doncaster January 1938 Grantham January 1941	Grantham March 1939 King's + February 1941	Doncaster March 193 Grantham April 1957
No 60004	King's + Aberdeen June 1962	G'Head February 1938 Haymarket September 1962	Heaton June 1940 Aberdeen June 1963	Haymarket July 1941
No 60005	G'Head	St. Margaret's October 1963	Aberdeen November 1963	
No 60006	King's + St. Margaret's October 1963	Grantham April 1938 Aberdeen April 1964	King's + April 1944	New England June 1963
No 60007	King's + November 1937 St. Margaret's October 1963	Grantham April 1944 Aberdeen July 1964	King's + June 1950	New England June 1963
No 60008	Doncaster September 1937 Grantham April 1957	King's + September 1937 King's + September 1957	Grantham December 1939 New England June 1963	King's + June 1950
No 60009	Haymarket June 1937	Aberdeen May 1962		
No 60010	King's + May 1937 Aberdeen October 1963	Grantham April 1957	King's + September 1957	New England June 1963
No 60011	King's + June 1937	Haymarket March 1938	Aberdeen June 1962	
No 60012	Haymarket June 1937	Dalry Road September 1963 (for storage)	Aberdeen January 1964	
No 60013	King's + King's + June 1950	Haymarket July 1937	King's + March 1938	Grantham May 1948
No 60014	King's + King's + May 1950	Grantham August 1944	King's Cross May 1948	Grantham June 1948
No 60015	King's + King's + September 1951	G'Head December 1936	King's + January 1937	Grantham April 1944
No 60016	King's + G'Head January 1945	G'Head November 1935 St. Margaret's October 1963	Heaton November 1939 Aberdeen November 1963	Heaton May 1943
No 60017	King's +	New England September 1963		

No 60018	G'Head December 1937 G'Head November 1945	Heaton October 1940	G'Head March 1943	Heaton May 1943
No 60019	Heaton	G'Head March 1943	St. Margaret's October 1963	Aberdeen November 1963
No 60020	G'Head	Heaton November 1944	G'Head October 1945	
No 60021	King's + King's + August 1944	Doncaster May 1939 Grantham March 1948	King's + August 1941 King's + June 1950	Grantham October 1943 New England June 1963
No 60022	Doncaster	Grantham October 1943	King's + April 1948	
No 60023	King's + St. Margaret's October 1963	Haymarket February 1938 Aberdeen May 1964	Heaton August 1941	G'Head January 1942
No 60024	Haymarket Haymarket May 1939	King's + July 1937 Dalry Road September 1963	Haymarket January 1938 St. Margaret's December 1963	Doncaster March 1939 Aberdeen May 1965
No 60025	Haymarket Grantham April 1950	King's + March 1939 King's + March 1950	Grantham April 1948 New England June 1963	King's + March 1950
No 60026	Haymarket Doncaster October 1947 New England June 1963	G'Head October 1937 King's + November 1947	Haymarket January 1938 Grantham April 1948	King's + March 1939 King's + September 1951
No 60027	Haymarket	St. Rollox May 1962	St. Margaret's September 1964	
No 60028	Haymarket Haymarket March 1939	G'Head March 1937 King's + May 1939	Haymarket February 1938 Grantham October 1945	Doncaster March 1939 King's + May 1948
No 60029	G'Head King's + October 1943	Doncaster January 1938 New England June 1963	King's + February 1938	G'Head August 1943
No 60030	Doncaster Grantham October 1942	King's + September 1937 King's + June 1950	Grantham December 1939 Grantham April 1957	King's + July 1942 King's + September 1957
No 60031	Haymarket	November 1937	St. Rollox February 1962	
No 60032	Doncaster Grantham October 1943	Grantham September 1938 King's + June 1950	King's + September 1938 New England June 1963	Doncaster May 1939
No 60033	King's +	Grantham April 1944	King's + March 1948	
No 60034	Doncaster New England June 1963	King's + July 1942 St. Margaret's October 1963	Grantham October 1942 Aberdeen May 1964	King's + April 1948

Above: No 60011 Empire of India on an express in November 1962. (CR/KMF)